Light and Sound

KINGFISHER

LONDON & NEW YORK

Copyright © Kingfisher 2012
Published in the United States by Kingfisher,
175 Fifth Ave., New York, NY 10010
Kingfisher is an imprint of Macmillan Children's Books, London.
All rights reserved.

Distributed in the U.S. and Canada by Macmillan,
175 Fifth Ave., New York, NY 10010

First published as *Kingfisher Young Knowledge: Light and Sound* in 2007
Additional material produced for Kingfisher by Discovery Books Ltd.

Library of Congress Cataloging-in-Publication data has been applied for.

ISBN: 978-0-7534-6779-4

Kingfisher books are available for special promotions and premiums.
For details contact: Special Markets Department, Macmillan,
175 Fifth Ave., New York, NY 10010.

For more information, please visit www.kingfisherbooks.com

Printed in China
1 3 5 7 9 8 6 4 2

1TR/1211/UTD/WKT/140MA

Note to readers: the website addresses listed in this book are correct at the time of going to print. However, due to the ever-changing nature of the Internet, website addresses and content can change. Websites can contain links that are unsuitable for children. The publisher cannot be held responsible for changes in website addresses or content or for information obtained through a third party. We strongly advise that Internet searches should be supervised by an adult.

Acknowledgments

The publisher would like to thank the following for permission to reproduce their material. Every care has been taken to trace copyright holders. However, if there have been unintentional omissions or failure to trace copyright holders, we apologize and will, if informed, endeavor to make corrections in any future edition.
b = bottom, *c* = center, *l* = left, *t* = top, *r* = right

Cover all images courtesy of Shutterstock.com; 1 Alamy/Stockbyte; 2–3 Corbis; 4–5 Corbis/Zefa; 6–7 Getty/Stone; 7 Science Photo Library (SPL)/Larry Landolfi; 8*l* Corbis/Randy Farris; 9*tr* Getty/Stone; 9*bl* Natural History Picture Agency/James Carmichael Jr.; 10–11 Alamy/Stock Connection; 12*c* Corbis/Walter Hodges; 12–13 Corbis/Zefa; 13*t* Nature Picture Library/David Shale; 14 Corbis; 15*t* Getty/Stone; 15*b* SPL; 16 Corbis/Aaron Horowitz; 17*t* SPL/Celestial Image Co.; 17*b* Nature Picture Library/Jorma Luhta; 18–19 Corbis; 19*tl* Alamy/Phototake Inc.; 20 Corbis/RoyMorsch; 21*t* Alamy/Imageshopstop; 21*b* SPL/Lawrence Lawry; 22 Getty/Photographer's Choice; 23*t* Alamy/Sami Sarkis; 23*b* SPL/NASA; 24 Brand X Pictures; 25*t* Corbis/NASA; 25*b* SPL/Custom Medical Stock Photo; 26 Alamy/Oote Boe; 27*t* SPL/Merlin Tuttle; 27 SPL; 28 Alamy/A. T. Willett; 28*t* Alamy/Imagestate; 30–31 Alamy/Butch Martin; 31*c* Corbis/Zefa; 32*br* Getty/Imagebank; 32–33 Corbis/Zefa; 33*t* Getty/Imagebank; 34 Corbis/Bill Ross; 35*bl* Getty/Imagebank; 35*r* Corbis/Carmen Redondo; 36 Frank Lane Picture Agency/David Hosking; 37 Corbis; 37*br* Getty/Photodisc Red; 38 Getty/Johner Images; 39*tl* Alamy/Profimedia; 39*b* Getty/Photonica; 40*l* Photolibrary.com; 40*r* Corbis; 41*t* SPL/Hank Morgan; 41*b* SPL/NASA; 48*t* Shutterstock/xtrekx; 48*b* Shutterstock/Dhoxax; 49 NASA; 52 Shutterstock/HerrBullermann; 53*t* Wikimedia/NASA; 53*b* Wikimedia/Eric Rolph; 56 Shutterstock/Llike

Illustrations on pages: 8, 30 Sebastien Quigley (Linden Artists); 10, 11 Encompass Graphics

Commissioned photography on pages 42–47 by Andy Crawford
Thank you to models Darius Caple, Jamie Chang-Leng, Mary Conquest, and Georgina Page

Light and Sound

Dr. Mike Goldsmith

KINGFISHER

NEW YORK

Contents

6 World of light

We need light to live. It gives us day and night, colors, pictures, stars, and rainbows. We also use it to play CDs and make electricity.

The bright Sun

The Sun is a star. It is a huge ball of burning gas that gives us light and warmth. Without it, there would not be any life on Earth.

Looking at the stars

Using telescopes, scientists can see more light from the stars. They can figure out how far away from Earth they are, how hot they are, and what they are made of.

Eyes and seeing

People need light to be able to see. Many nighttime animals need less light to see than we do. They have big eyes that take in as much light as possible.

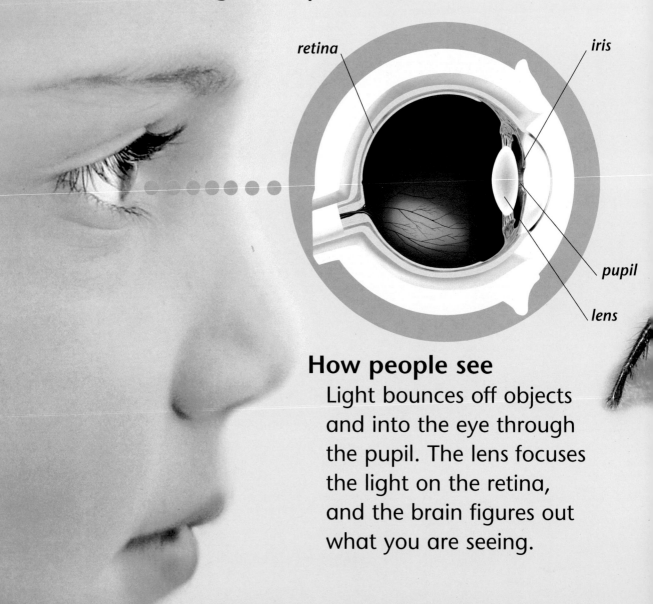

retina

iris

pupil

lens

How people see

Light bounces off objects and into the eye through the pupil. The lens focuses the light on the retina, and the brain figures out what you are seeing.

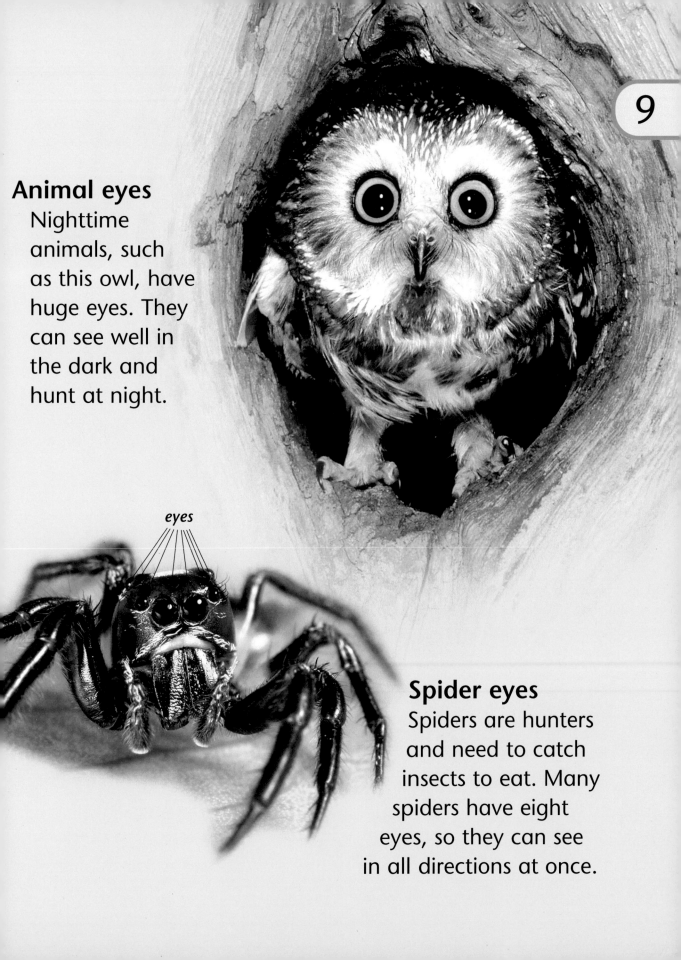

Animal eyes

Nighttime animals, such as this owl, have huge eyes. They can see well in the dark and hunt at night.

eyes

Spider eyes

Spiders are hunters and need to catch insects to eat. Many spiders have eight eyes, so they can see in all directions at once.

Color

People can see millions of different colors. Colors mix in different ways—all pigments mixed together make black, and all colors of light mixed together make white.

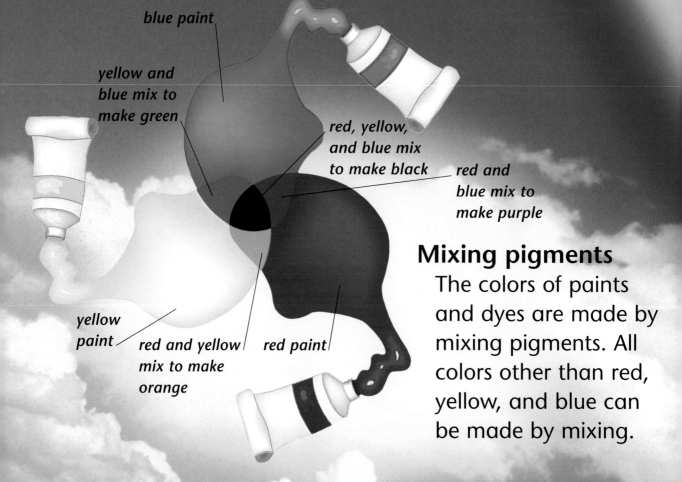

blue paint

yellow and blue mix to make green

red, yellow, and blue mix to make black

red and blue mix to make purple

yellow paint

red and yellow mix to make orange

red paint

Mixing pigments

The colors of paints and dyes are made by mixing pigments. All colors other than red, yellow, and blue can be made by mixing.

green light

red light

blue light

green and red mix to make yellow

blue and green mix to make cyan

all colors of light mixed together make white

red and blue mix to make magenta

Mixing lights

Lights mix in a different way to pigments. All colors are made by mixing different amounts of red, blue, and green light.

Separating light

Sunlight (white light) is a mixture of colors. Raindrops separate these colors to make a rainbow of red, orange, yellow, green, blue, indigo, and violet.

Making light

Anything will shine with light if it gets hot enough. Most of the light we see comes from hot objects, such as the Sun, light bulbs, and stars.

Electric light

Some substances glow with light when electricity passes through them. When electricity is passed through neon gas, it gives out colored light that can be used in advertising signs.

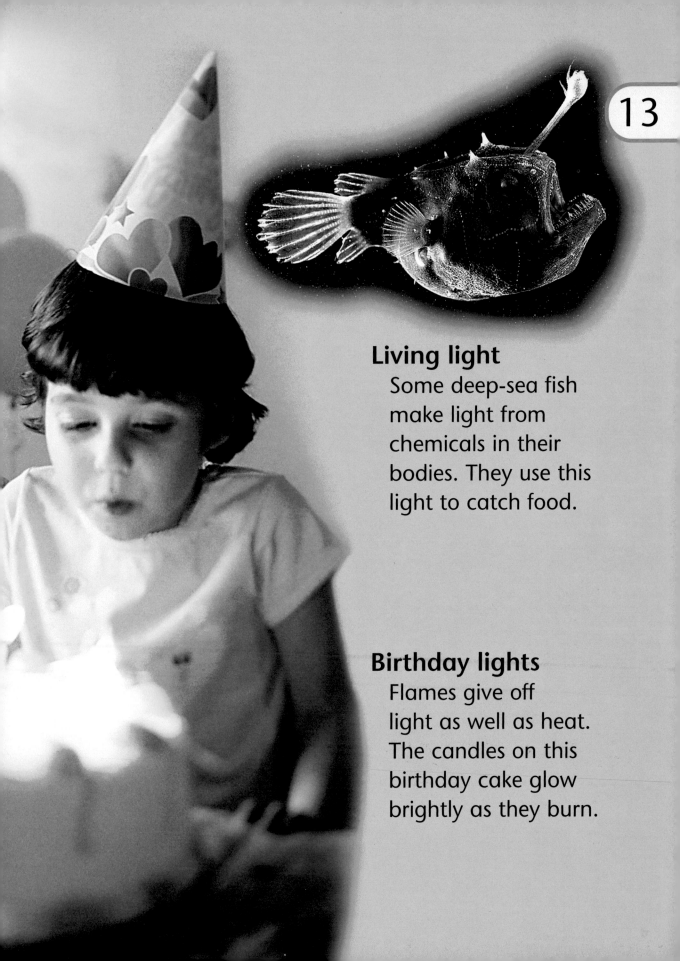

Living light

Some deep-sea fish
make light from
chemicals in their
bodies. They use this
light to catch food.

Birthday lights

Flames give off
light as well as heat.
The candles on this
birthday cake glow
brightly as they burn.

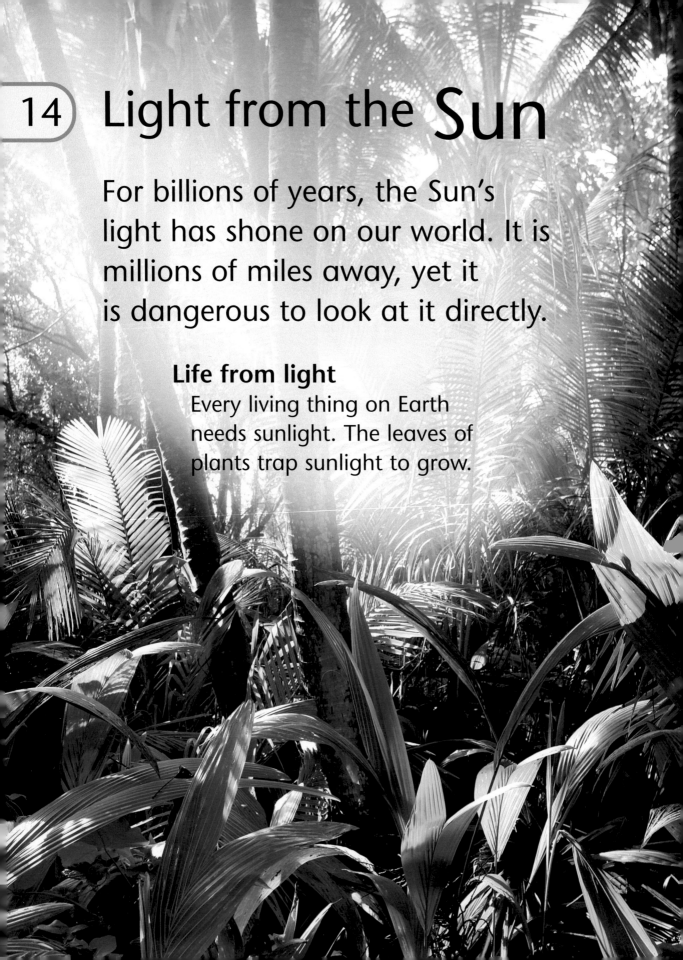

Light from the Sun

For billions of years, the Sun's light has shone on our world. It is millions of miles away, yet it is dangerous to look at it directly.

Life from light

Every living thing on Earth needs sunlight. The leaves of plants trap sunlight to grow.

Glowing sunsets

As Earth turns, the Sun moves across the sky. When the Sun is low in the sky, it looks red because its light passes through the thick, dusty air near the ground.

Staying warm

Heat from the Sun keeps Earth's oceans liquid. Without it, all of the water and air around the planet would be frozen.

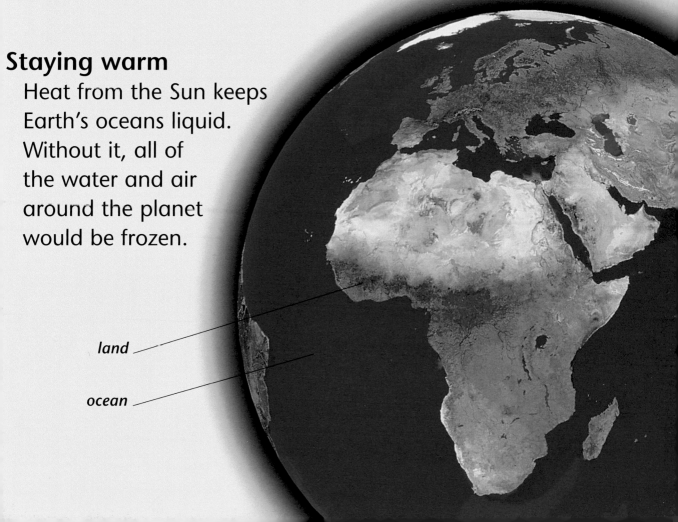

land

ocean

Darkness and light

When there is no light, we see darkness. Our planet spins in space—when it turns away from the Sun, it is night. We need other sources of light to see in the dark.

Moonlight
The Moon does not make its own light. Sunlight bounces off it and makes it glow.

Stars

Stars make their
own light. Many are
brighter than our star,
the Sun. They look
very faint because
they are so far away.

Nature's light show

The Sun sends out particles
that carry electricity. These
can bounce off particles
in the air, making the sky
glow with different colors.

Shadows

When something blocks light, it casts a shadow. It is cooler and darker in shadows because they are cut off from the Sun's warmth and light.

In the shade

All solid objects cast shadows. They may be long or short, depending on how sunlight falls on them.

Darkness by day

Sometimes the Moon passes between Earth and the Sun. It blocks our view of the Sun, causing darkness. This is called a solar eclipse.

Bouncing light

Light bounces off most objects. A lot of light bounces off snow, so it shines brightly in sunlight. Coal hardly lets any light bounce back from it, so it is dark.

Seeing double

The surface of a mirror is so smooth that it bounces back light in exactly the same pattern as it receives it. This is called a reflection.

Bright night

In this picture, the Sun's light has bounced off the Moon to the ocean, making the water shine with light.

Talking with light

Light can travel through glass threads called optical fibers. These fibers can carry telephone calls and computer signals.

Bending light

Objects that light can travel through are called transparent. When light enters a transparent substance—such as glass or water—it bends.

Funny shapes

When light travels between water and air, it bends, and what we see seems out of shape. The bending light has made this boy's body look bigger in the water.

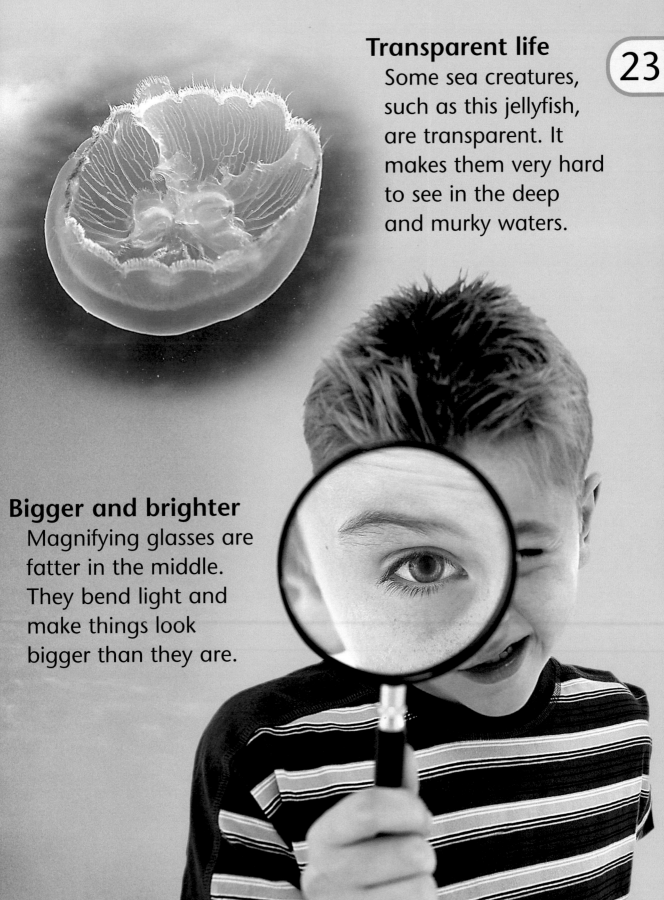

Transparent life

Some sea creatures, such as this jellyfish, are transparent. It makes them very hard to see in the deep and murky waters.

Bigger and brighter

Magnifying glasses are fatter in the middle. They bend light and make things look bigger than they are.

Electric light

Light can make electricity, and electricity can make light. In a light bulb, electricity heats up a thin wire so that it glows.

Light bulbs

By coloring the glass of these light bulbs, different colored lights are produced. Light bulbs get hot when turned on, so do not touch them.

Solar power
Solar panels outside
this space station
collect sunlight and
turn it into electrity.
The electricity is then
used as power.

Laser surgery
Very narrow beams
of light, called lasers,
can be used for many
things. They are used
for delicate operations,
such as eye surgery.

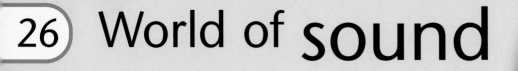

World of sound

There are sounds all around us. We listen to music and hear voices. Sound has many other uses, too. It can "draw" pictures and help animals find their prey.

Unwelcome sounds
Sounds that are unpleasant to listen to, such as the sound of heavy drills, are called noise.

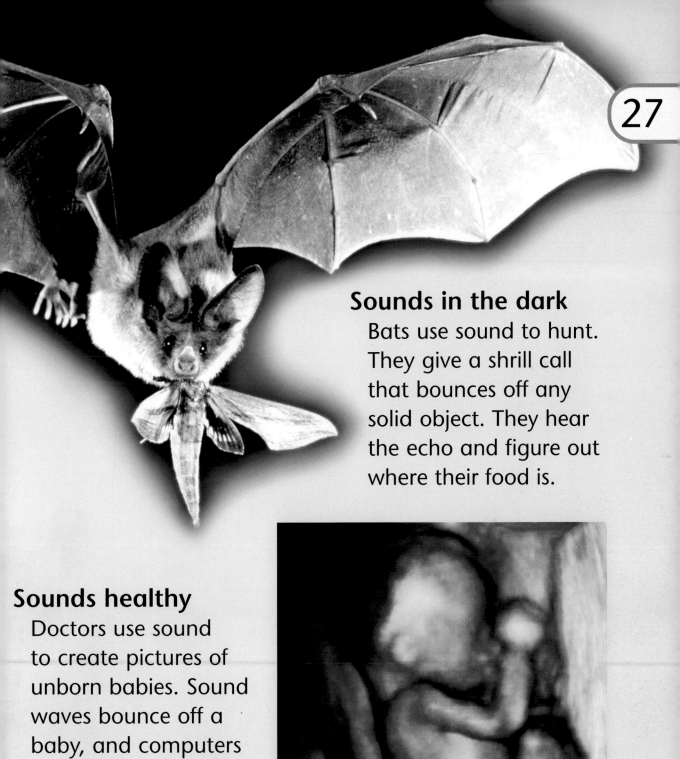

Sounds in the dark

Bats use sound to hunt. They give a shrill call that bounces off any solid object. They hear the echo and figure out where their food is.

Sounds healthy

Doctors use sound to create pictures of unborn babies. Sound waves bounce off a baby, and computers can "draw" the picture.

What is sound?

Sound is a type of wave, or ripple. Like ripples in a pond, sound travels in all directions. Sounds get quieter the farther you are from their source.

Boom!
Some planes travel faster than sound. They make a shock wave in the air. This can be heard as a loud bang called a sonic boom.

Silent space

Sound can travel through air or water. There is no air or water in space, so there is no sound.

Sound speeds

Sound travels quicker through water than through air. These killer whales use clicks and whistles to communicate underwater.

How do we hear?

When sound enters the ear, it travels down a tube. The tube's end is covered by a very thin wall of skin called the eardrum.

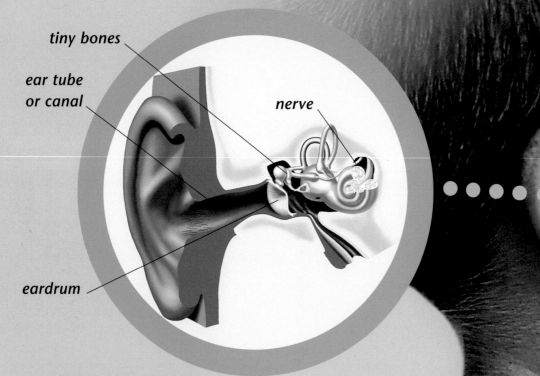

tiny bones

ear tube or canal

nerve

eardrum

Inside the ear

When a sound hits the eardrum, it wobbles and makes the tiny bones inside the ear vibrate.

Hearing

Nerves in the ear send
messages to the brain.
The brain figures out what
sound is being heard.

Animal ears

Most animals can hear, but
few have ears like ours. The
fennec fox has huge ears
that can turn around to pick
up the slightest sound.

Making sound

Sound is usually made when something moves back and forth very quickly. The moving thing might be a leaf in the breeze, the inside of a bell, or a guitar string.

Musical sounds

Blowing a trumpet makes a buzzing sound in the mouthpiece. This sound travels through the trumpet to make music.

Voices

When you speak or sing, two flaps of skin in your throat wobble. These are called vocal cords.

Snaps and crackles

Sound can be a burst, such as a balloon popping or fireworks exploding. We hear the crackles and fizzes while watching the lights.

How sound travels

Sound travels as waves through air, water, or solid objects. The waves die away eventually, but they can cover great distances at first.

Long journeys

A busy street is a noisy place. The sounds of people talking and cars and other vehicles can travel a long way.

Echoes

Sound waves
bounce back from
hard objects, such as
walls. We call these
sounds echoes.

*The echo bounces
off the cave wall
and the same shout
is heard again.*

child shouts

Quiet or loud?

The more a sound wave wobbles, the louder it sounds. One of the loudest natural sounds is when a volcano erupts. Bombs and rocket engines make the loudest human sounds.

Shh . . .

Some animals can hear sounds that are too quiet for people. An aardvark can hear termites crawling under the ground.

Ouch!

Very loud sounds can damage your ears. Our ears tense up when they hear loud noises, making everything sound muffled.

High or low?

Sound waves wobble at different speeds.
The faster a sound wave wobbles,
the higher the sound it produces.
Sounds that wobble slower are lower.

Making music

Violin strings move
quickly and make a high
sound. Most guitar strings
move more slowly, so
their sound is lower.

High meows and low roars

Kittens have small vocal cords and weak lungs, so they make high, quiet meows. Lions are big cats with powerful lungs. They make low, loud roars.

Electric sound

Sound can be changed into electricity. The electricity can then be changed back into sound again. This happens when you talk on the telephone.

Microphones

A microphone changes sounds into a wobbling pattern of electricity. A loudspeaker turns these patterns back into sounds.

loudspeaker

microphone

Changing sound

By turning sounds into pictures like this one, scientists can see what we hear. These pictures are called sonograms.

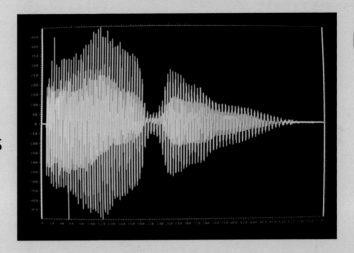

Voices from space

When astronauts are outside a spacecraft, they communicate using microphones and loudspeakers.

Shadow puppets

Make animal puppets

Solid shapes block the light and cast shadows. You can make different shaped shadows, such as this dragon, and put on a shadow-puppet show.

You will need:
- Pencil
- Colored paper
- Scissors
- Candy wrappers
- Tape
- Drinking straw or stick
- Flashlight

Draw a dragon with a long, pointed tail, feet, and an open mouth on colored paper.

Carefully cut out the dragon using scissors. Ask an adult to help if needed.

On one side, stick on candy wrappers to make flames coming out of the dragon's mouth.

You can make other shadow puppets, such as a cat or a bird.

4

Tape a drinking straw or short stick to the back. Turn the dragon over and draw an eye, nose, and wings.

5

In a darkened room, ask a friend to shine a flashlight onto a plain wall. This will make shadows.

Position your shadow puppet in front of the flashlight and move it around in the light.

Shadow clock

Tell the time by shadows

Shadow clocks measure time using shadows cast by the Sun. Have fun making your own clock.

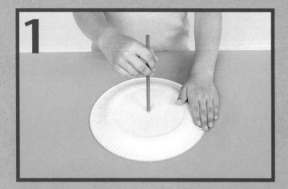

Make a small hole in the middle of a paper plate and stand a drinking straw upright in the hole.

You will need:
- Paper plate
- Drinking straw
- Colored markers

Keep your clock in the same place, and when the shadows fall, you'll be able to tell the time.

Put the plate in a sunlit place. Every hour, draw a line along the shadow that the straw makes and note the time.

Xylophone

Make music

You can create a simple xylophone using glasses of water and a wooden spoon.

You will need:
- 5 glasses, all the same size
- Pitcher of water
- Food coloring
- Wooden spoon

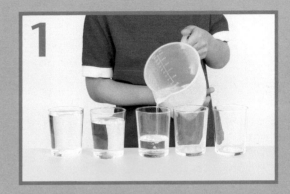

Line up the glasses and pour water into them. Fill the first up to the top and then the rest with a little less water than the one before.

You can add a few drops of different food coloring to the glasses to color the water.

Gently tap each glass with the spoon and you will hear that each one makes a different sound.

Plastic-cup telephone

Make a working phone

You can make sound travel along a piece of stretched-out string. The plastic cups work as the microphone and the loudspeaker so that you can hear what your friend is saying.

You will need:
- 2 plastic cups
- Stickers and colored paper
- Scissors
- Modeling clay
- Sharp pencil
- Piece of string, 11–20 ft. (4–6 m) long

1

Decorate two clean, empty plastic cups with stickers and shapes cut out from different colored paper.

The sound of your voice travels along the string.

2

Place a ball of modeling clay under each cup and make a hole in the bottom with a sharp pencil.

3

Thread one end of the string through the hole and then tie a knot at the end.

4

Do the same with the other cup. Give a friend one cup and stretch out the string. Talk into the cup.

If your friend holds the other cup to his ear, he will hear what you are saying.

Glossary

blocks—gets in the way of

chemical—substance used in chemistry

communicate—to send a message to another creature

damage—to hurt or cause injury

delicate—easily broken or damaged

echo—a sound that bounces off an object

frozen—turned to ice

gas—a shapeless substance, such as air, that is not solid or liquid

iris—the colored part of the eye

liquid—a runny substance

loudspeaker—a device that changes electricity into sound

lungs—the parts inside the body that are used for breathing

magnifying—making something seem bigger than it is

mouthpiece—a part that goes over or into the mouth

natural—occurring in nature; not made by people or machines

neon—an invisible gas that glows when electricity passes through it

nerves—special fibers that run from the brain to all parts of the body

optical fiber—a thin thread of glass along which light can pass

particles—extremely small pieces

pigments—substances that give something its color

prey—an animal that is hunted and killed by another animal

produce—to make or create

produced—made

reflection—the image you see when you look in a mirror, glass, or very clear, still water

retina—a special layer at the back of the eye that picks up light

separating—splitting apart

solar—having to do with the Sun

solar eclipse—when the Moon passes between Earth and the Sun and causes darkness

solar panel—a panel that collects sunlight and turns it into electricity

sonic boom—the noise created when something travels faster than sound

sonogram—a computer-generated picture of a sound

source—where something comes from; for example, the Sun is a source of light

telescope—an invention that makes things that are far away appear closer

transparent—see-through, or clear

vehicles—machines used for transporting people or things

vibrate—to move rapidly back and forth

vocal cords—flaps of skin that enable humans to speak

The content of this book will be useful to help teach and reinforce various elements of the language arts and science curricula in the elementary grades. It also provides opportunities for crosscurricular lessons in math and art.

Extension activities

Spoken language/codes
Morse code is a way of communicating using off-and-on sounds or lights. You'll find the code at *www.enchantedlearning.com/ morsecode/notopad.shtml.* Use either tapping sounds or flashes from a flashlight to practice sending messages to a friend.

Creative writing
1) Find a quiet place and sit there for 5–10 minutes and simply listen. Write down the different sounds that you hear. Write about the experience in the form of a poem.

2) What if you woke up one morning to find that you could hear ten times as well as you normally do—and no one knew?

Write a short story about your adventures that day.

Science
The content of this book relates to the scientific themes of energy, light, and sound. Other specific links to the science curriculum include astronomy (pp. 6, 12, 14–15, 16–17); diversity (pp. 8–9, 13, 23, 31, 39); structure and function (pp. 8–9, 13, 23, 27, 29, 30–31, 33, 36, 39); technology (pp. 7, 12, 21, 23, 24–25, 27, 40–41); and transfer of energy (p. 14).

On p. 34, you read that sound travels as waves through air, water, or solid objects. Which is louder? Sit at one end of a table. Ask a friend to sit at the other end and use a metal spoon to tap out a short message to you in Morse code. Then put your head on the table, with one ear resting on the surface. Ask the friend to repeat the message. What do you observe?

Crosscurricular links
1) *Science and technology/ oral language:* Technology is advancing so rapidly that soon

it will be hard to find light bulbs like those described on p. 24. Instead, we are using CFL (compact fluorescent lamp) bulbs and LEDs (light-emitting diodes). Both types use far less energy because they do not get as hot. Research to find out more about CFLs and LEDs. Present a short talk to tell others what you've learned, including which kind of light bulb you think is best to use and why.

2) Art: On pp. 10–11, you read about mixing pigments to make different colors of paints and dyes. Now is your chance to see this for yourself! Divide the contents of a can of white frosting into thirds, placing each on its own paper plate. Add a few drops of yellow food coloring to the first and mix it with a spoon until the entire clump of frosting is yellow. Do the same with red coloring on the second plate and then again with blue coloring on the third. Experiment with mixing small amounts of colored frosting together and see what different colors you can create.

Using the projects

Children can do these projects at home. Here are some ideas for extending them:

Pages 42–43: Experiment with your hands in front of the light. What animal shapes can you make?

Page 44: Be your own shadow clock! Early in the morning, go to a paved area with lots of room. Stand in the middle and have someone use chalk to draw an outline of your feet. Then ask them to draw an outline of your shadow. Go back every hour and stand exactly in your footprints while your partner outlines your shadow. Watch how your shadow changes shape and size as the position of the Sun changes.

Page 45: Try this activity using bottles. Blow over the neck of each bottle to get a note.

Page 46–47: What happens if you coat the string with modeling clay?

Did you know?

- One of the loudest sounds on record is a blue whale singing.

- Doctors use optical fibers to see inside patients' bodies.

- John Cage wrote a piece of music called *4'33"*. It is four minutes and 33 seconds of no music at all, so the audience can listen to the other sounds around them.

- There is no sound in space. Astronauts have to use radios in their helmets to communicate with one another.

- The body of a glowworm contains chemicals that make light.

- Dolphins and bats use sounds to make a "picture" of their surroundings so that they can hunt for food.

- Before glass mirrors were invented, the Romans and Greeks used polished bronze to see their reflections.

- Lightning strikes Earth around 100 times every second.

- The sperm whale uses powerful bursts of sound to stun and kill its prey.

- In a thunderstorm, you can see lightning before you hear thunder. This is because light travels faster than sound.

- You can tell the time of day using shadows. Shadows are short in the middle of the day, when the Sun is high up in the sky. In the early morning or late afternoon, the Sun is near the horizon, and shadows are much longer.

- When you turn on an old-fashioned light bulb, only ten percent of the electricity used is changed into light. The rest is wasted as heat.

- Fish have ears inside their bodies. They make noises to find out where they are, to listen for enemies, and even to find food.

- One of the loudest human-made sounds is that of a rocket blasting off. Once it enters space, however, it is silent because there is no air.

- The smallest bone in your body is in your ear. It is called the stapes (stirrup) bone and is only 3.3 millimeters long.

- On the Moon, the sky is black because there is no air to scatter the light.

- The speed of light is the fastest thing we know—it travels at about 186,000 mi. (300,000km) per second. It takes light about eight minutes to reach Earth from the Sun.

- Some grasshoppers have ears on their legs.

- Sound travels around four times faster through water than it does through air.

- Rainbows form when sunlight shines through millions of raindrops.

Light and sound quiz

The answers to these questions can all be found by looking back through the book. See how many you get right. You can check your answers on page 56.

1) What color is made if you mix red and blue?
   A—Green
   B—Orange
   C—Purple

2) If all colors of light are mixed together, what color do they make?
   A—Black
   B—White
   C—Cyan

3) Without heat from the Sun, Earth's oceans would what?
   A—Stay as they are
   B—Freeze
   C—Change color

4) Why is part of Earth dark at night?
   A—It is facing away from the Sun.
   B—The Moon blocks the Sun.
   C—The Sun spins away from Earth.

5) What is it called when the Moon passes between Earth and the Sun?
   A—A lunar eclipse
   B—A solar eclipse
   C—A star eclipse

6) What do optical fibers carry along them?
   A—Light
   B—Water
   C—Heat

7) What do magnifying glasses do?
   A—Bend light to make things look smaller
   B—Make things look the same
   C—Bend light to make things look bigger

8) What are the flaps of skin in your throat that wobble when you sing or speak called?
   A—Larynx
   B—Tonsils
   C—Vocal cords

9) How does sound travel through the air?
   A—As waves
   B—As straight lines
   C—As long, curved lines

10) Which is the loudest sound?
    A—A volcano erupting
    B—A wave breaking
    C—A child shouting

11) What is the brightest light on Earth?
    A—A firework
    B—A light bulb
    C—The Sun

12) What is the word given to the image you see when you look in a mirror?
    A—A refraction
    B—A reflection
    C—A shadow

Books to read

Awesome Experiments in Light & Sound by Michael A. Dispezio, Sterling, 2006

Hands-on Science: Sound and Light by Jack Challoner, Kingfisher, 2012

Holt Science and Technology: Sound and Light, Holt McDougal, 2003

Light & Sound (Little Science Stars) by Clint Twist, TickTock, 2009

Light and Sound: What Makes Stuff Bright and Loud? (Check It Out), TickTock, 2005

Places to visit

American Museum of Science and Energy, Tennessee
www.amse.org
This wonderful museum contains some great exhibits, including Exploration Station, where you can explore light and sound, robotics, vision, and much more.

Mid-America Science Museum, Arizona
www.midamericamuseum.org
At this fun museum, you can experiment with science hands on; the exhibits encourage you to get involved. You can see how a camera works in the walk-in camera, explore optical illusions with mirrors, and even trap your own shadow in the Shadow Trapper!

New York Hall of Science, New York
www.nysci.org
Visit this fantastic museum, which has more than 450 permanent exhibits to explore. In the "Seeing the Light" exhibition, you can find out how the eye works, how shadows are created, and explore the world of optical illusions.

Websites

http://scifiles.larc.nasa.gov/text/kids/ D_Lab/acts_sound.html
Learn all about sound and find some interesting activities and experiments with sound on this NASA website.

www.brainpop.com/science
On this website, you can search for the topics of light and sound and watch videos to find out all about them. Discover how whales use sound to communicate and learn the two ways of creating artificial light.

www.sciencebob.com
There are some great ideas for science experiments on this website, including some based on sound and light. Make a duck call, view some optical illusions, and listen to chicken sounds from a cup! You can also ask Bob any science questions you can think of.

www.sciencemadesimple.com
This website contains fun science projects and experiments for you to do at home, as well as science articles and videos. Find out why the sky is blue and why leaves change color in the fall.

Light and sound quiz answers

1) C	7) C
2) B	8) C
3) B	9) A
4) A	10) A
5) B	11) C
6) A	12) B